Littleport
Colouring Book
2

Littleport Colouring Book 2
Copyright© 2017 Jean Shaw
All rights reserved
ISBN-13: 978-1979660013
ISBN-10: 1979660018

Jean Shaw lives in Littleport

If you would like your own personalised colouring book, please contact her on 07780365127

Visit her author page at
https://amazon.co.uk/Jean-Shaw/e/B001K8A1A0

THIS BOOK BELONGS TO

....

Set within the fenlands
Is the village I call home
Littleport's expanding fast
It certainly has grown

The locals are all friendly
And most will say "Hello"
They'll smile and pass the time of day
It wasn't always so

Back in the 1800's
That may not have been the case
For taxes led to riots
Causing havoc in the place

Some labourers went to prison
Five hung by their necks
Others went to New South Wales
Names changed to keep respect

Years have passed now senseless crime
Gives Littleport a name
Like vandalism, petty theft
By people with no shame

If punishments as years before
Were deportation, hanging, prison
These mindless individuals
Might have a different vision

Littleport's got a lot to offer
Has all the shops we need
Butcher, baker, grocer
Library for those who read

We have a new health centre
Optician, dentist too
Turf accountant if you want to bet
Tattoo parlour – yes that's true

(I wrote this poem a few years ago, BEFORE we lost our butcher, baker, bank, estate agent hardware store and wedding outfitter, so I apologise for it no longer being accurate.)

We've a handy bank, Post Office
And a useful launderette
Sports centre, pubs and garages
And free parking don't forget

Two local schools and playgroups
A drop in centre too
Chapels, Halls, St. George's Church
To suit your point of view

If you're looking for a carpet
Hardware or DIY
Special gift or wedding suit
Main Street's the place to try

We've restaurants and takeaways
For all who like to eat
Hairdressers and chiropodist
For bad hair or troubled feet

There's an accountant if you need one
Solicitors as well
And even estate agents
If you've a house to rent or sell

We've a very pleasant river
Fire station that's just fine
And a useful railway station
Which serves the London line

As transport links get better
The employment's not just farming
Industrial parks are growing up
With a speed that's quite alarming

But still we have the rich fen soil
And dark and fertile means
Sugar beet, potatoes, wheat
Barley, oats and beans

Historically there's been an annual show
Where produce was displayed
But development's meant the site has gone
So locals are dismayed

For people came from miles around
To celebrate the day
Even Harley riders
From as far as USA

Yes, Littleport has quite a lot
For a village it's okay
It's where I chose to make my home
And where I'll likely stay

©Jean Shaw

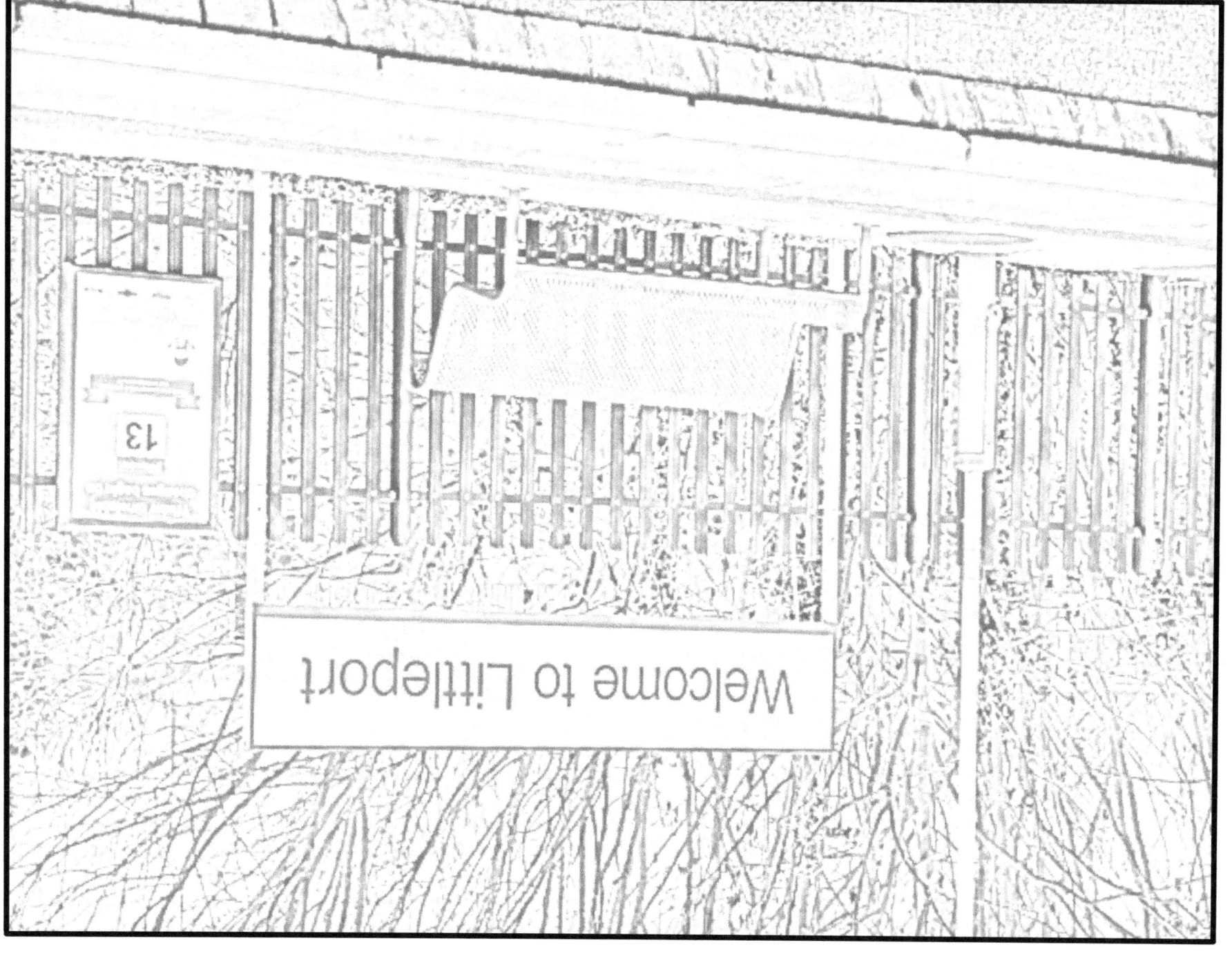

The following words can be found in the diagram below reading forward, backward, up, down and diagonally. Find the words and circle them.

fens	flood
doctors	wheat
village	tiger
history	shops
farmers	geese
island	shirts

```
F E N S R A Q Y L F L O O D I U
C W S O P Z P O B K M G R K W V
E W H I J G U L Q E A W H E I Q
F Q O Y A T V P I U E H X L W P
J C P G T Z L P H U W E L C G M
H I S L A N D G H T K A X Z G D
I A W Z T R O C M T G T Z I E O
S I I L P C L B S E T W O S E C
T V C B T B J V M H U M D H S T
O T G V I I S J I B I Q K I E O
R R C Z G R U O B M H X B R D R
Y A D E E J Y R R T E V N T K S
Q V U M R Y X D P H U S H S P G
I B R O F D R F G W P F N H Y R
C A L C S H W R E Z H M U Z T K
F G C L U I O M O V I E A W L Z
```

Each of these Cryptograms is a message in substitution code. THE SILLY DOG might become UJD WQPPZ BVN if U is substituted for T, J for H, D for E, etc. One way to break the code is to look for repeated letters. E, T, A, O, N, R and I are the most often used letters. A single letter is usually A or I; OF, IS and IT are common 2-letter words; try THE or AND for a 3-letter group. The code is different for each Cryptogram.

1. Brm Awbbamhdq Qwdbo smqm wc 1816

2. Ilr kda stkqckqhrtv   sx qkb z
   Lrtsizhr Orqitr

3. Uqbob rpob 215 ktseym qgtdbd yw
   Eyunebkqon yw 1900

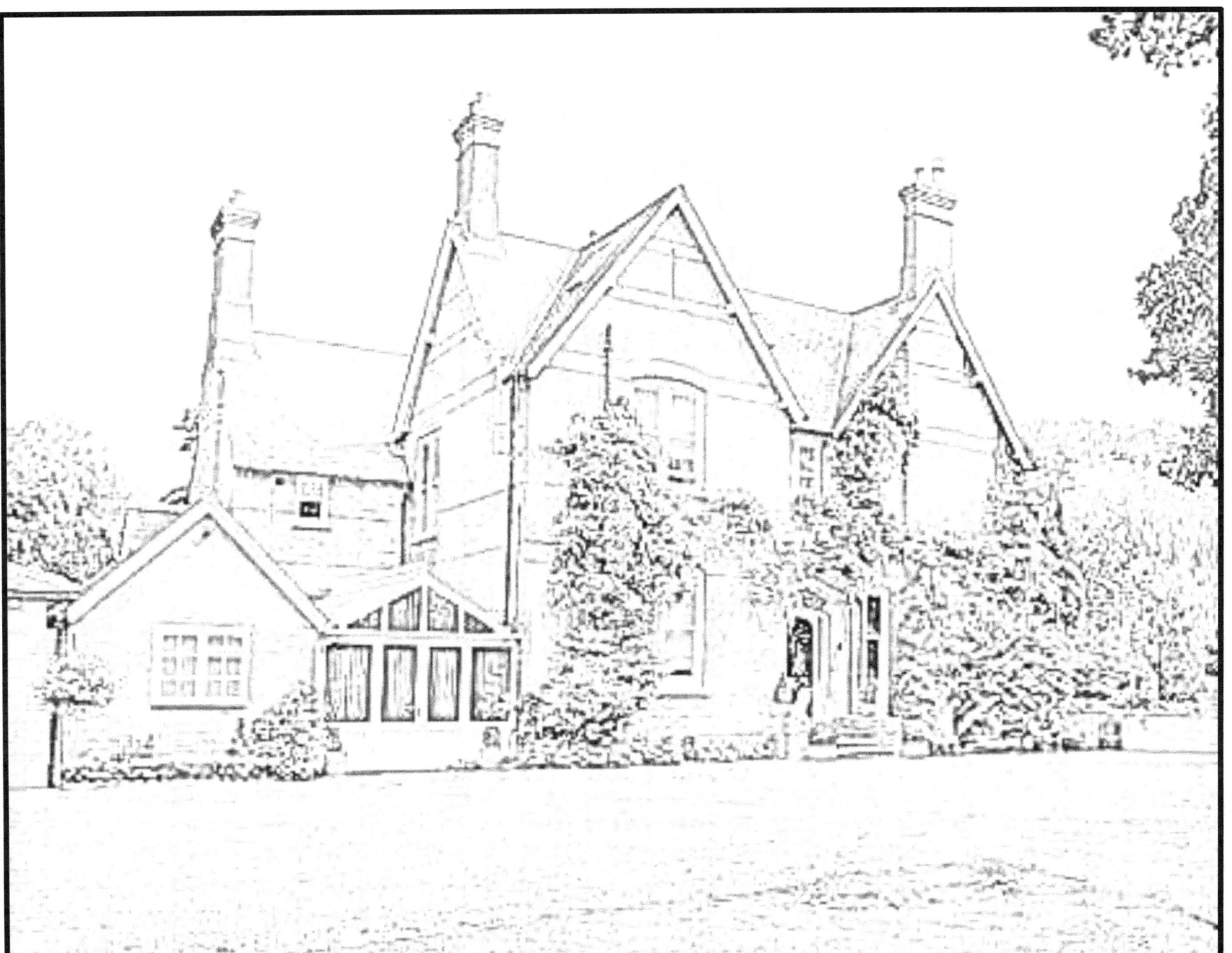

Insert a different letter of the alphabet into each of the 26 empty boxes to form words reading across. The letter you insert may be at the beginning, the end or the middle of the word. Each letter of the alphabet will be used only once. Cross off each letter in the list as you use it. All the letters in each row are not necessarily used in forming the word.

Example: In the first row, we have inserted the letter Z to form the word AZURE

A B C D E F G H I J K L M N O P Q R S T U V W X Y Z

K	T	E	R	U	**Z**	A	R	V	F	U	S
Y	X	C	N	E	B	T	A	T	S	E	I
X	L	S	R	O	T		O	D	N	S	R
X	T	S	T	A	O		E	S	U	O	H
K	B	T	E	B		A	G	U	S	G	Y
Y	T	I	N	U	M		O	C	M	F	R	L
D	Z	A	X	J	P		O	O	L	F	V	Z
O	Z	S	K	R	O		H	C	T	I	P	M
Y	R	L	E	W	E	D	M	A	W	A	X	Z
A	T	S	I	M	E		C	U	V	A	W	K
K	R	E	R	I	U		C	A	V	L	T
A	E	G	R	O	E		T	S	I	Z	S	Y
O	K	Y	T	I	R		H	C	H	J	L	T
L	M	O	Y	A	W	I	A	R	O	C	P
G	C	W	H	O	S		C	O	D	X	V	B
W	O	D	L	A	U		N	A	U	A	S	N
Z	D	Z	W	G	N		A	E	H	W	T	J
Z	O	P	Y	X	E		E	B	G	C	M	R
J	D	X	M	S	R		T	C	A	R	T	D
W	L	D	S	N	A		S	X	N	B	K	M
C	N	K	S	N	O		N	O	G	O	N	V
O	J	O	S	N	A		A	R	A	C	S	Y
N	T	Y	E	G	N		L	L	A	H	C	B
S	O	N	J	O	J		R	O	T	C	A	F
J	T	S	U	A	H		E	U	C	V	B	T
A	T	R	A	N	S		O	E	T	R	Y

Each of these Crypto Words are writen in substitution code. SILLY might become WQPPZ if S is substituted for W, I for Q, L for P, etc. When you have identified a word, use the known letters to decode the other words in the list.

HINT: w=a

1. ALWPA = _____

2. HUQWHK = _____

3. EMWIIDPND = _____

4. DPNXPDDHXPN = _____

5. QXNDH = _____

6. HXUQA = _____

7. AQNDUHND = _____

8. CUQUHEKEID = _____

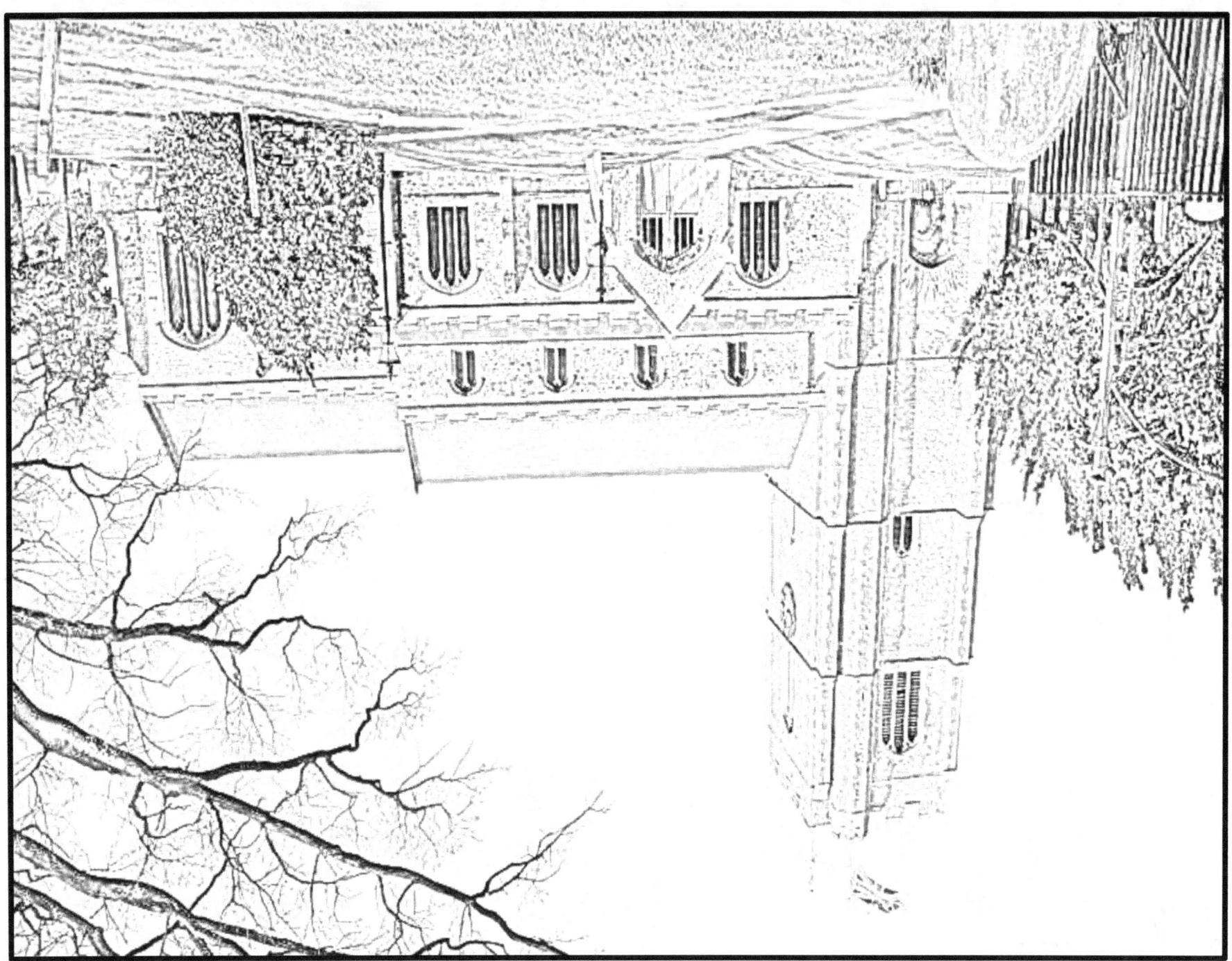

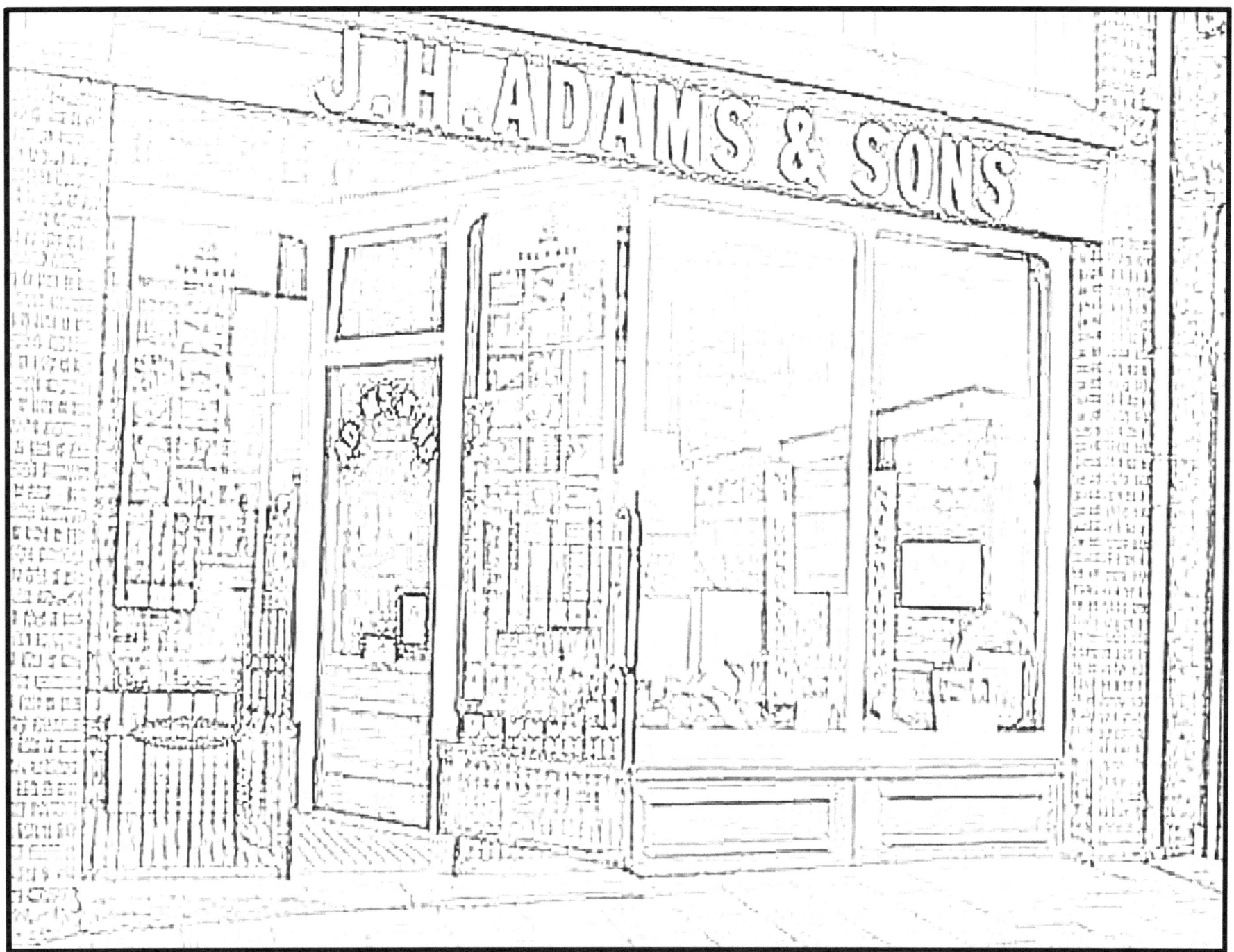

The spaces between the words in the following message have been eliminated and divided into pieces. Rearrange the pieces to reconstruct the messages. The dashes indicate the number of letters in each word.

```
INT LPY TTI OYE IDE PLE TDE
DSI HTO OEP TAC TRO GNU PEL
```

_ _

_ _ _ _ _ _ _ _ _ _ _ _ _ _ _ _ _ _ _ _

_ _ _ _ _ _ _ _ _ _ _

_ _ _ _

Each of these Crypto Words are writen in substitution code. SILLY might become WQPPZ if S is substituted for W, I for Q, L for P, etc. When you have identified a word, use the known letters to decode the other words in the list.

HINT: w=a

1. ALWPA =

2. HUQWHK =

3. EMWIIDPND =

4. DPNXPDDHXPN =

5. QXNDH =

6. HXUQA =

7. AQNDUHND =

8. CUQUHEKEID =

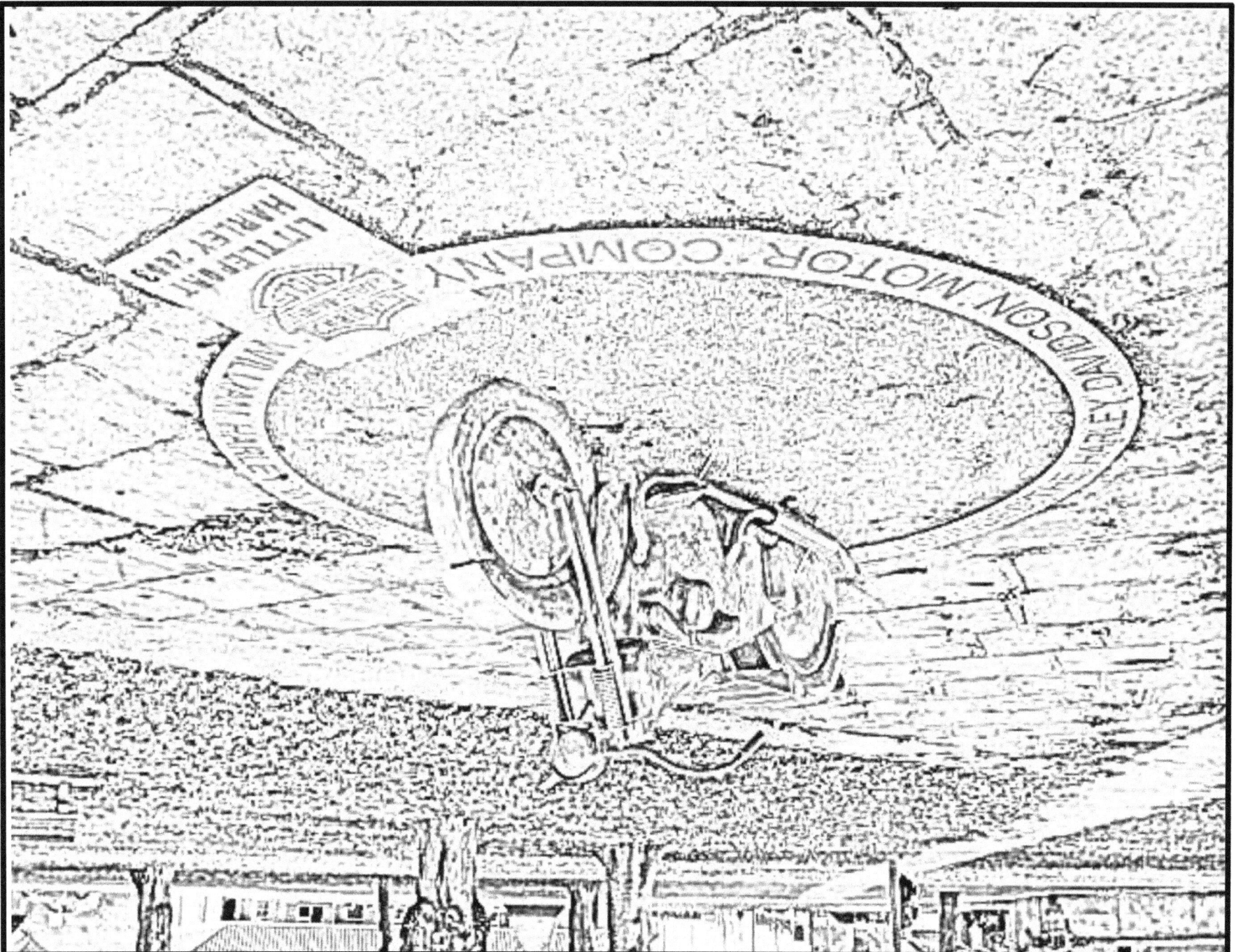

Place a number in each empty box so that each row, column, and nine-box square contains the numbers 1 to 9.

2	6	1					4	9	
9	7			4	6				
					2	6			
1				5		9	4	6	
	2			6	9			5	
	9	6				8	1		
3		2	4	8					
		4				2		3	
7						1	5		

The spaces between the words in the following message have been eliminated and divided into pieces. Rearrange the pieces to reconstruct the messages. The dashes indicate the number of letters in each word.

```
WOR ACT GUS INL KIN KIN BAN
ATT EDT HEH OPE ORY DUR NED
OBE ITT URS TAL SHI ORT GHO
RTF LEP ING
```

_ _ _ _ _ _ _ _ _

_ _ _ _ _ _ _ _ _ _ _

_ _ _ _ _

_ _ _ _

_ _ _ _ _ _ _ _ _

_ _ _ _ _ _ _

_ _ _

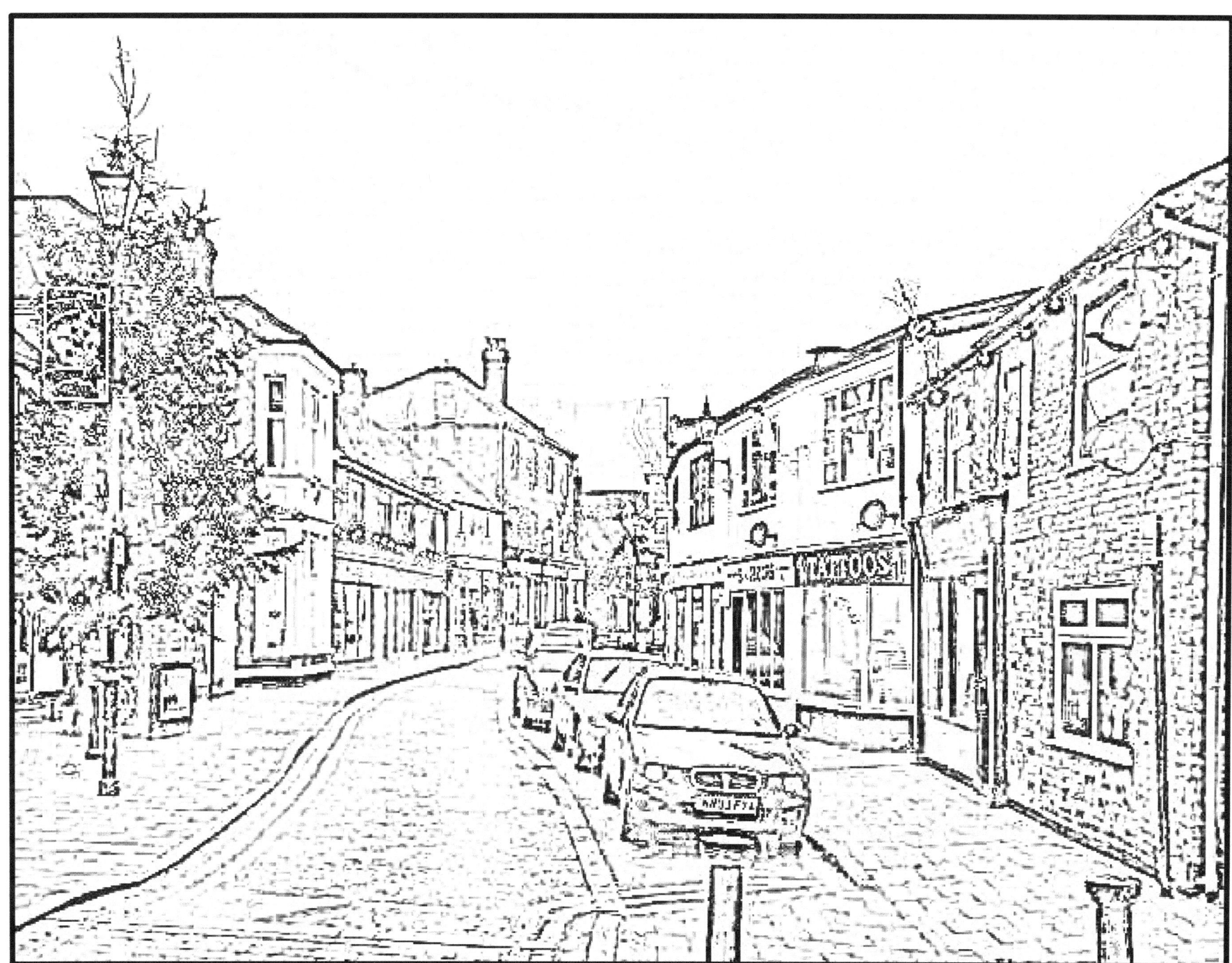

The below messages are in a number code based on how text messages are formed on a 'flip phone'. Each number represents one of the letters shown on the picture of the phone to the left. You must decide which one. A number is not necessarily the same letter each time.

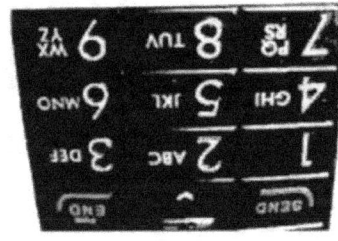

1. 843 8455243 7446 927 6744462559 3662833 86 843 94 46 1984

2. 46 1947 54885376783 423 2 8377425 35663

Enter a single letter in each blank square in the diagrams below to form interlocking answers, each of which spell out distinct common words that differ only by the given pairs. See the example below to get a better idea. With the given arrangement of letters and blanks HOLE and HOST can be formed. More than one pair of words may appear to be possible, however the interlocking word will help eliminate the possibilites.

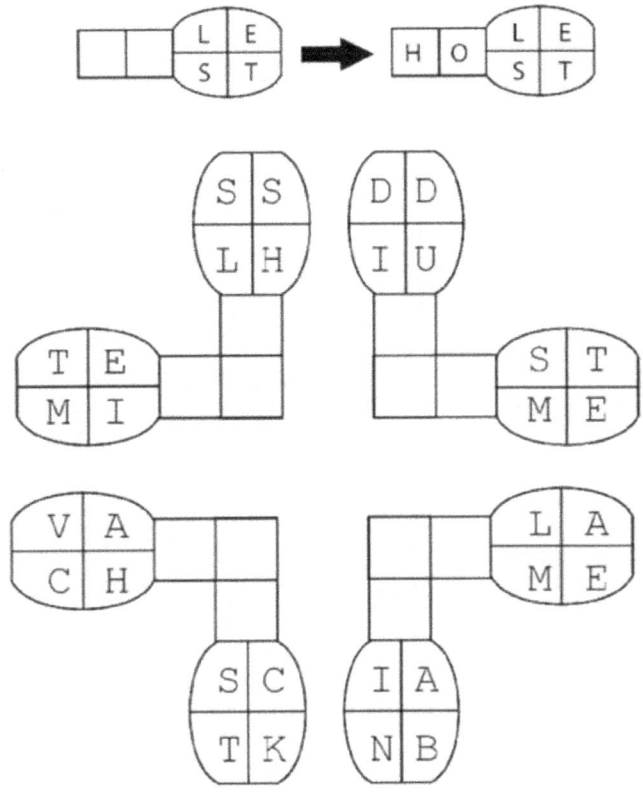

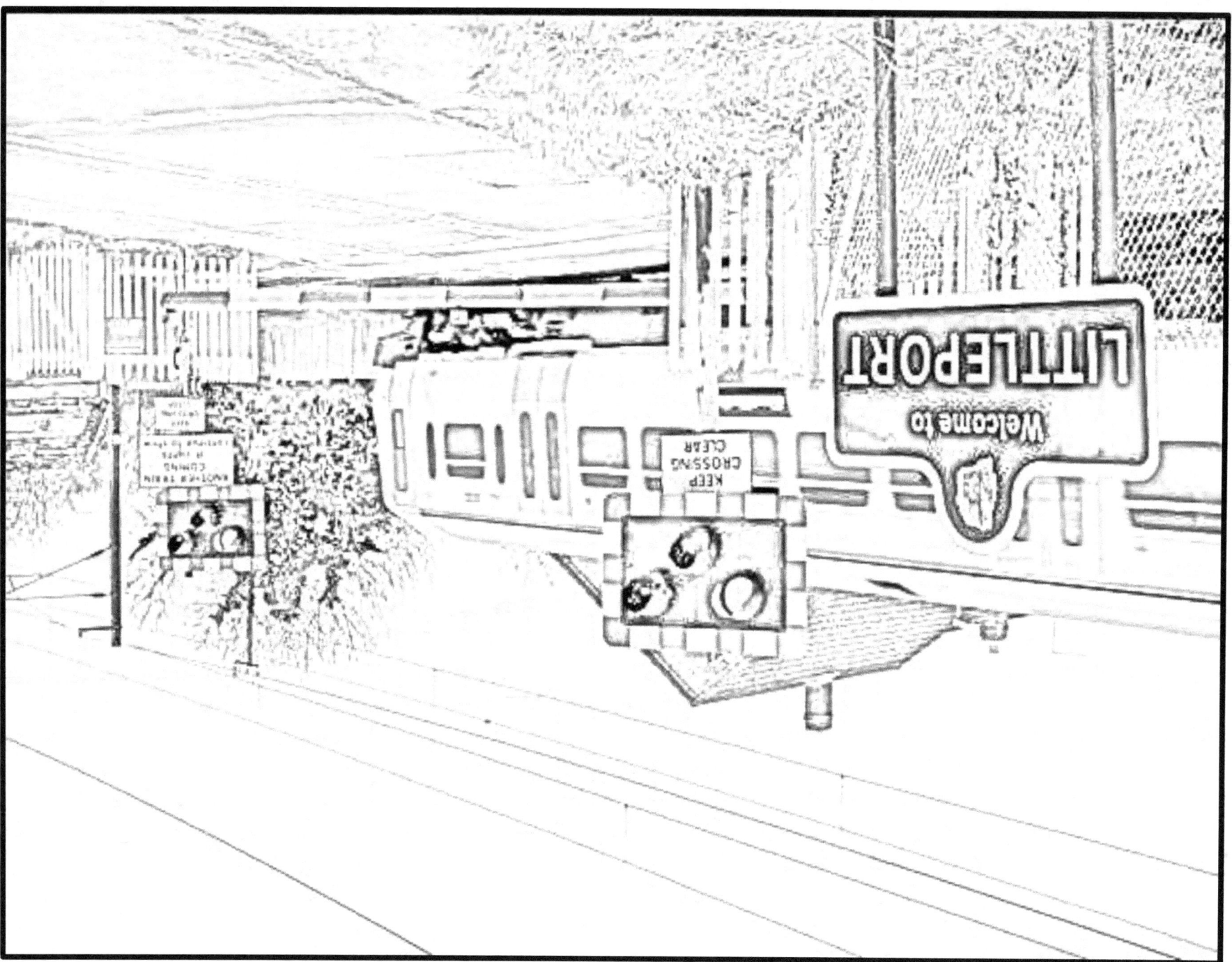

For this puzzle, only five of the eight words given wil fit together in the diagram. Fill each circle with one letter so that the words read in the directions indicated by the arrows.

norm	moot
trot	toon
trim	golf
toot	nine

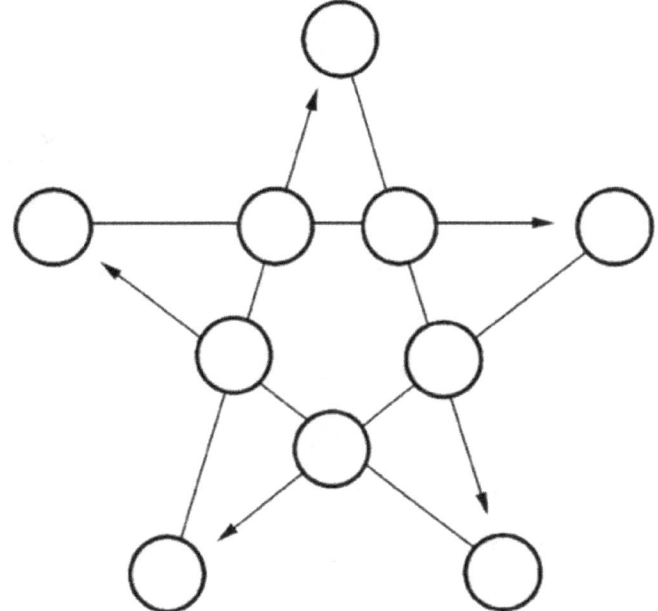

Fill in the diagram with the 5-letter answers to the clues. The numbers before the clues tell you where each word begins and ends. When completed, the line down the center of the diagram will spell out another word.

1 to 3: not clean
2 to 4: room under roof
4 to 6: large group of singers
5 to 7: a translucent quartz

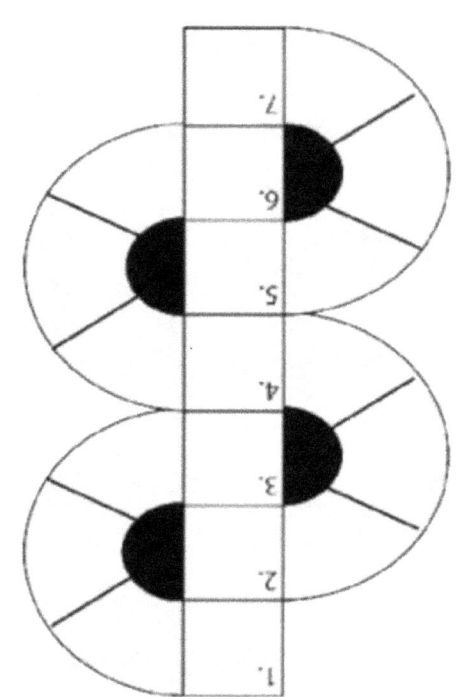

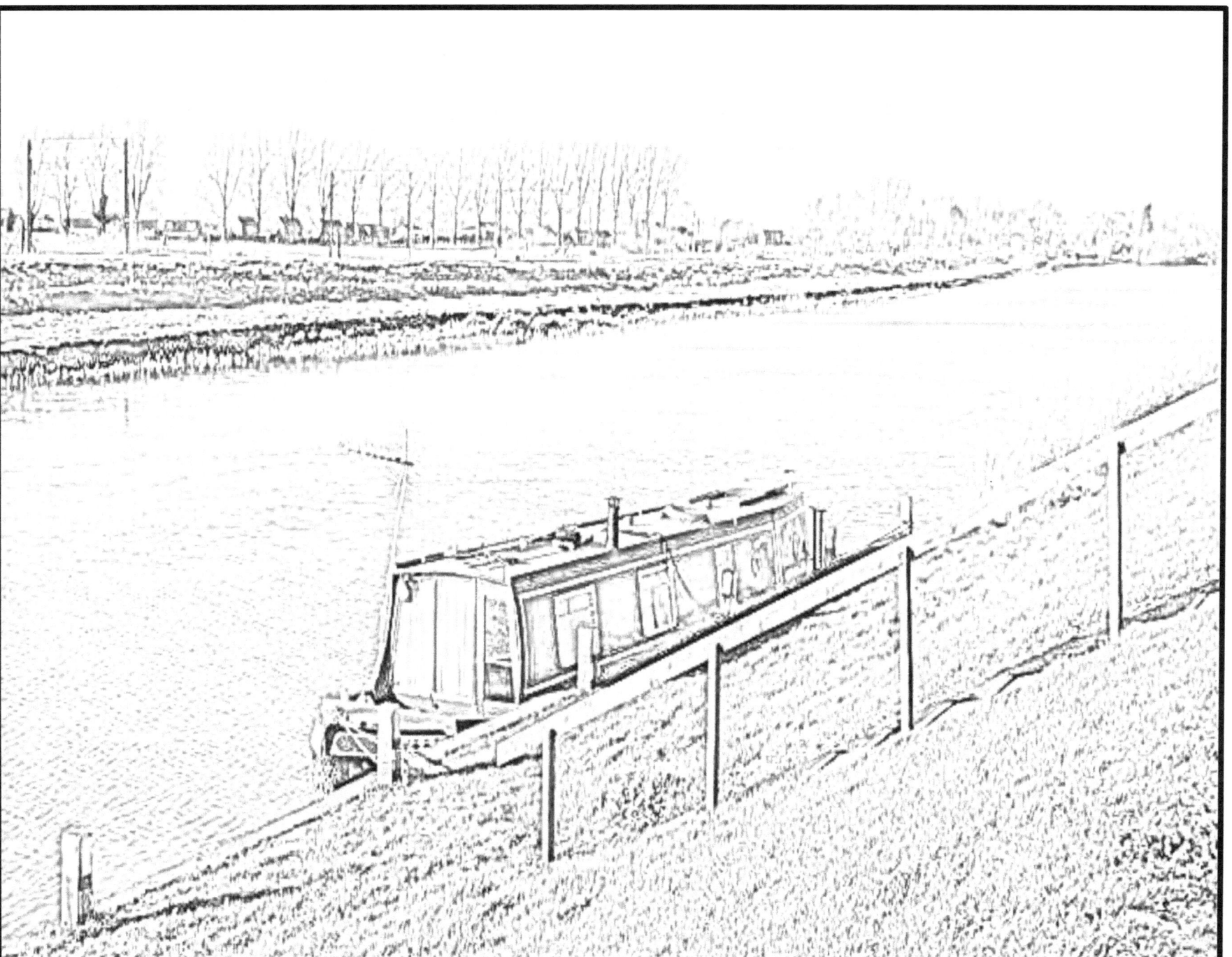

The following words can be found in the diagram below reading forward, backward, up, down and diagonally. Find the words and circle them.

chemist   statue
leisure   geese
littleport   church
talking   trial
silver   shops
annual   hope

```
P C I L L T E R O T H Y M
L T H Y O H C R U H C M J V
E D M E Y U X S P O H S V T N
S F Y X M S J J K B Ö V W F M
E G Ö T R I A L D W M E
E S A D B K S P U M O N H I
G T O E T I Z Y W W D F O G O
O G E M W B R Ö N G U C G B E G H
U T D H G E M L C U R H X Ö I B
S R E N G K V A K G X T L H
E E C M Y U V C S N T V W B Y
U V W X E N M Ö C L D I K C M A
T L A U N N A X M U Y K D R R
A I W C B G V R W A E U J L N
T S K B N S J Ö K C R N U
S C H T E L S U R E G Ö Ö H T
```

Place a number in each empty box so that each row, column, and nine-box square contains the numbers 1 to 9.

4				7			3	
	2	3		9		4	7	5
5							9	
						3	1	
		9	7		3	2	8	
7		4	1				5	
			3	1		5	6	
	5		4		9		2	
3	6					1	4	

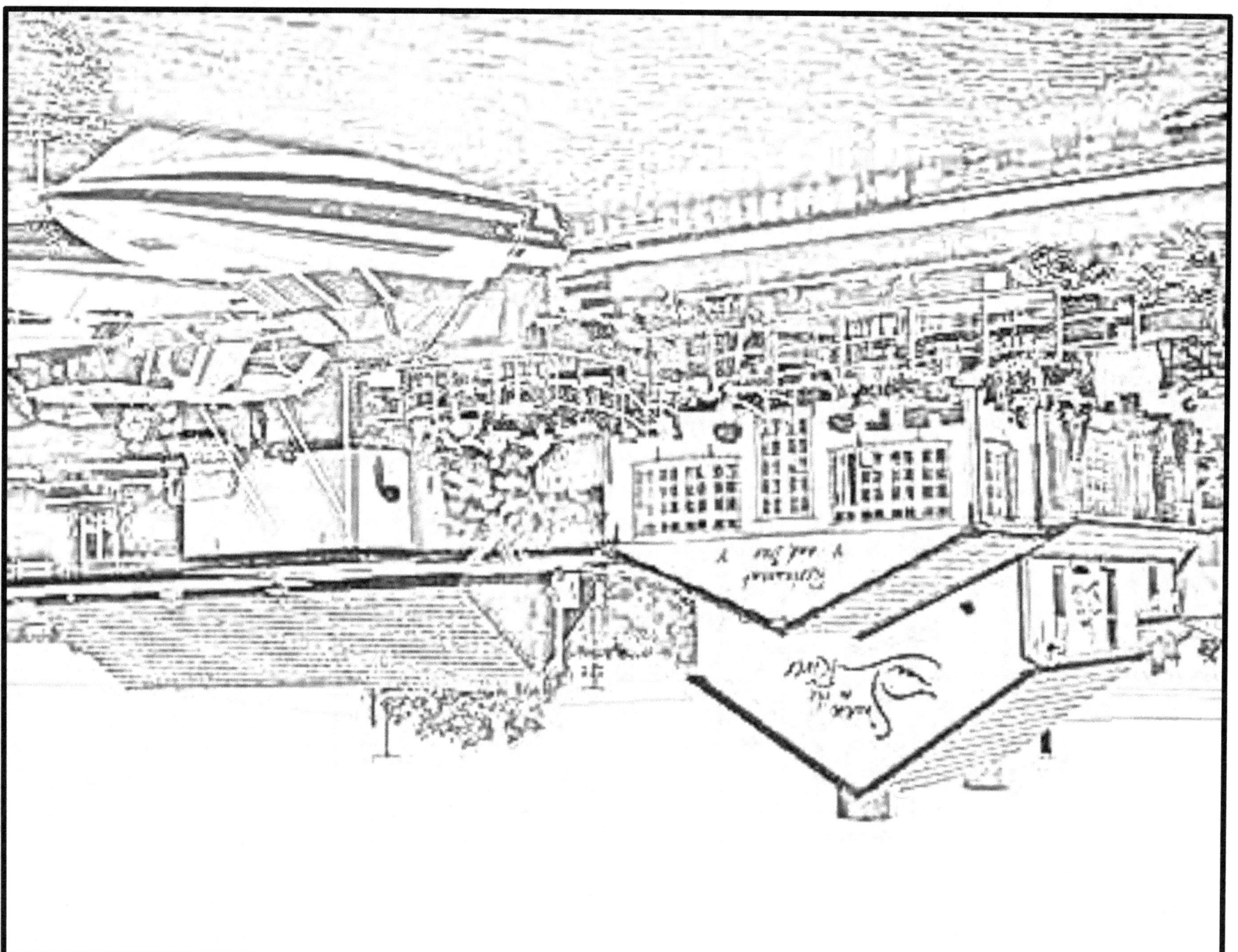

Following are puzzles that will challenge your sense of logic. Choose the answer that best fits the question. Think the questions through - some of the questions are tricky!

1. In a certain code-language, CUL, WAP, DIR means red little box, SUT; MAD BIX, means well arranged pile, BIX, FAC, DIR means pile of boxes. What is the code for "of here is"?

    A: FAC
    B: SUT
    C: DIR
    D: BIX

2. In a family there is a husband, wife, two sons and two daughters. All the ladies were invited to a dinner. Both sons went to the park to play. The husband did not return home yet from office. Who was left at home?

    A: Only the wife was at home
    B: All the ladies were at home
    C: Only the sons were at home
    D: Nobody was at home

Following are puzzles that will challenge your sense of logic. Choose the answer that best fits the question. Think the questions through - some of the questions are tricky!

1. Following is the bus for route for Bus Number 10. Buses on this route generally go to Connaught Palace. We are inferring that this bus goes to the Connaught Place. Choose the correct inference:

   A: The inference is definitely true
   B: The inference is definitely false
   C: The inference can not be drawn

2. If in a code language, COULD is written as BNTKC and MARGIN is written as LZQFHM, how will MOULDING be written in that code?

   A: NITKHOMF
   B: CIMFLNTK
   C: LNKTCHMF
   D: LNTKCHMF

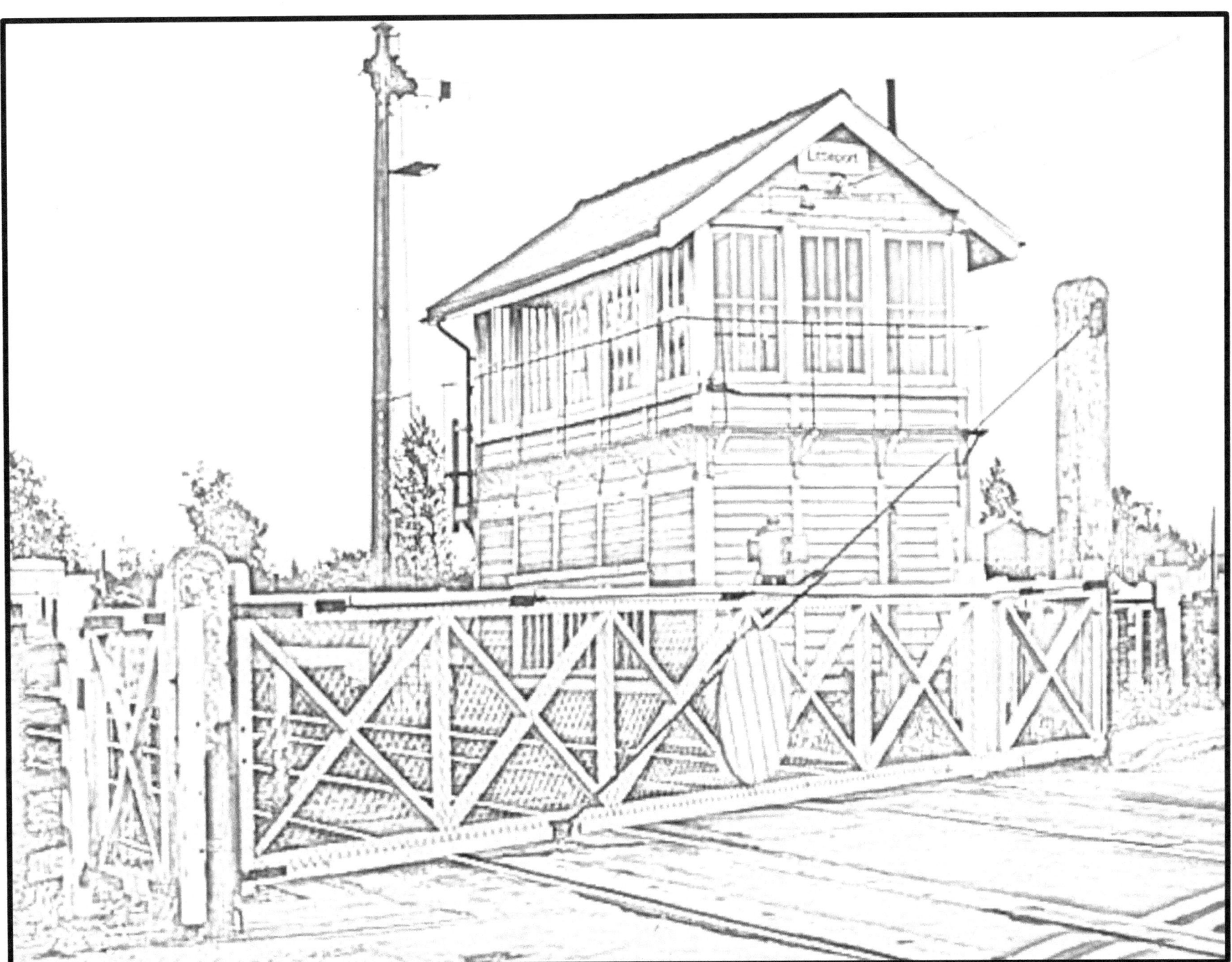

Ten common English words have been split apart and scattered throughout the diagram. Your quest is to locate the correct first letter for each word and then follow the given course throughout the diagram to spell the correct answer. The code for the direction indicates the number of spaces the next letter will jump in the diagram, and the direction the letter will go. Each letter will be used only once. The first answer has been provided.

NOTE: To locate the starting letter for each word, it is helpful to look at the direction of the following letter to see how far from the top, bottom, or sides of the diagram you must look. For example, if the direction of the second letter is 4N, the first letter must be in the bottom row, otherwise it would be impossible to go north by 4 spaces.

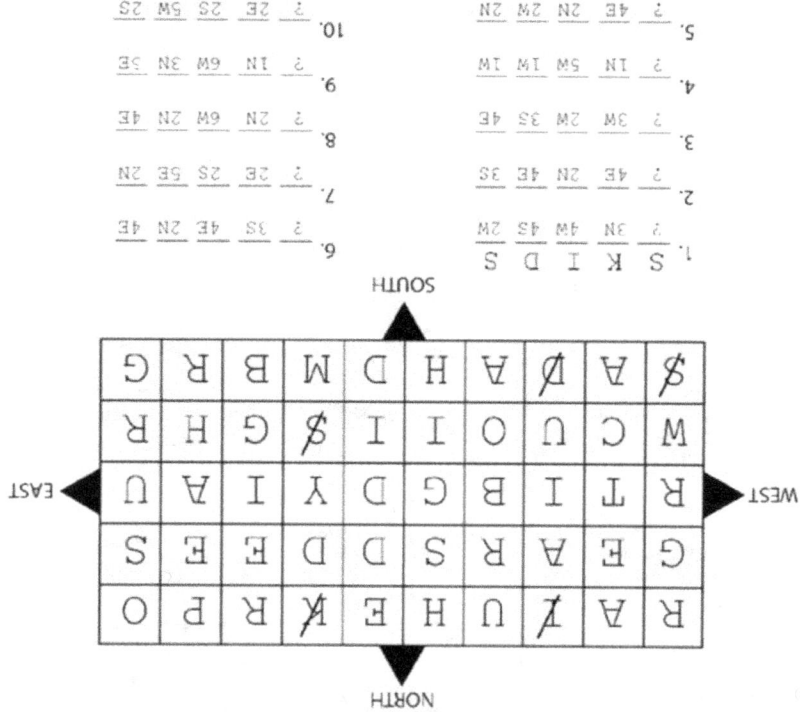

1. S K I D S
   ? 3N 4W 4S 2W

2. ? 4E 2N 4E 3S

3. ? 3W 2W 3S 4E

4. ? 1N 5W 1W 1W

5. ? 4E 2N 2W 2N

6. ? 3S 4E 2N 4E

7. ? 2E 2S 5E 2N

8. ? 2N 6W 2N 4E

9. ? 1N 6W 3N 5E

10. ? 2E 2S 5W 2S

The following words can be found in the diagram below reading forward, backward, up, down and diagonally. Find the words and circle them.

timebank	rural
talking	fens
factory	barber
onions	boats
shops	river
charity	church

```
S H O P S P H X N R U R A L H B
H Z F Z R M R V E A Y K M K T T
C B E H J S N Q S B K R Q S A P
F O N I O N S E Z Q L Y Q L D T
A K S I Y P I W Z U H R K T W I
C J A F B O W T Q H L I H Z A M
T L Y R X X H A H P N V Z W X E
O W W S D B Q O N G Q E T O E B
R Q I U X O T C X U N R W L B A
Y K T T L A Y A I K X G G C A N
U Y K K N T X B H L G X T H R K
B U N D I S S I Q O U B H U B N
M I W R W F D C A B M L O R E K
N V A V T T P U O C Y G K C R O
U H E Q B S C J O Y P R B H Q T
C O B I Y P E T I X I D L L B R
```

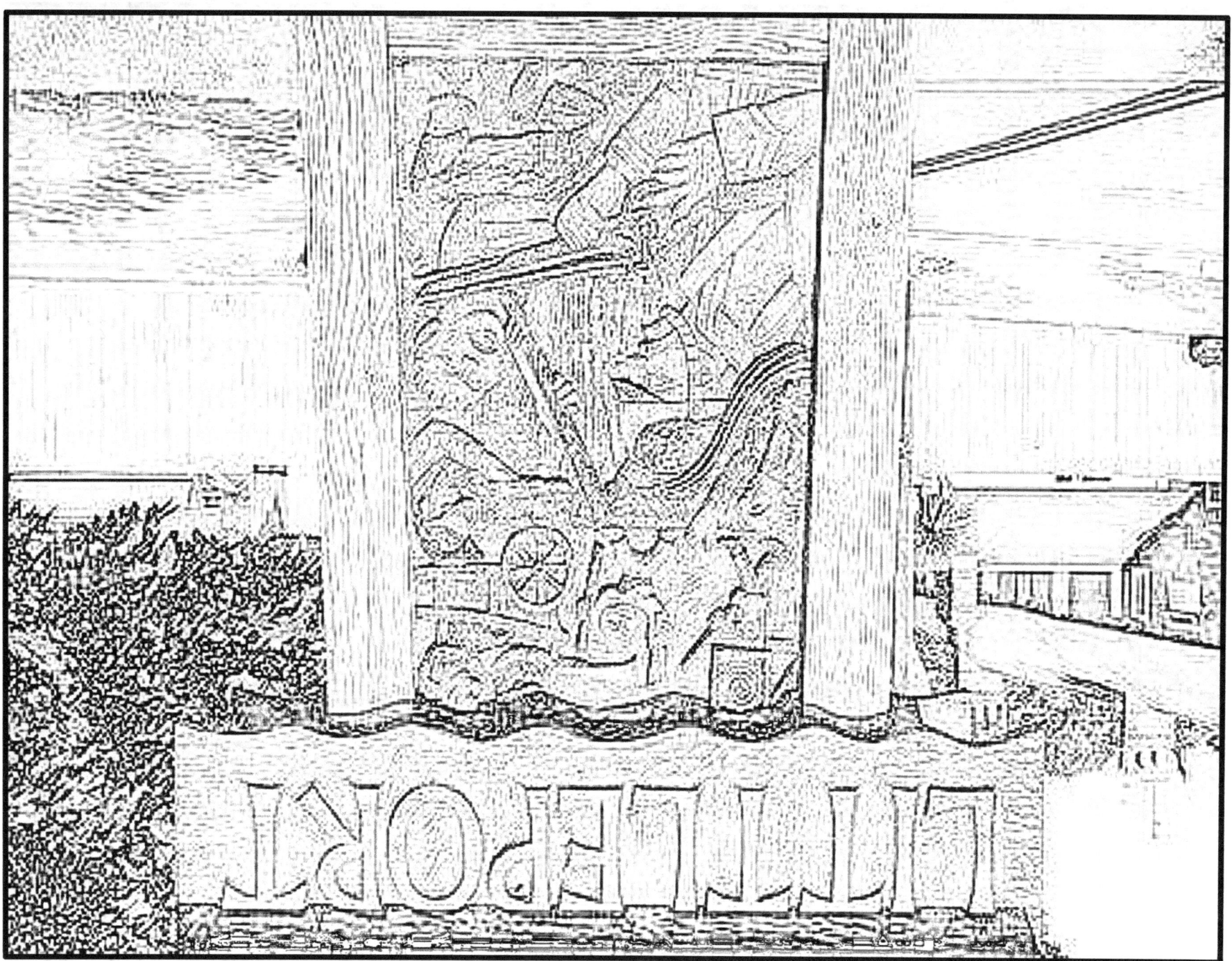

Find your way through the maze starting from the opening labeled START and coming out of the maze at the opening labeled FINISH.

Place a number in each empty box so that each row, column, and nine-box square contains the numbers 1 to 9.

				1			7	5
				4				2
			9	6			1	3
		3		2				
	4						2	
9	6	2	5	4			8	7
6	1	4	7	8				
8		4		5				
7			9			1		

Following are puzzles that will challenge your sense of logic. Choose the answer that best fits the question. Think the questions through - some of the questions are tricky!

1. In a military code, CAUTION is coded as UACITNO. How will you write MISUNDERSTAND?

    A: SIMUNEDSRTAND
    B: SIMNUEDSRATDN
    C: SMIUNDERSTAND
    D: None of the above

2. Ms. Forest likes to let her students choose who their partners will be; however, no pair of students may work together more than seven class periods in a row. Adam and Baxter have studied together seven class periods in a row. Carter and Dennis have worked together three class periods in a row. Carter does not want to work with Adam. Who should be assigned to work with Baxter?

    A: Carter
    B: Adam
    C: Dennis
    D: Forest

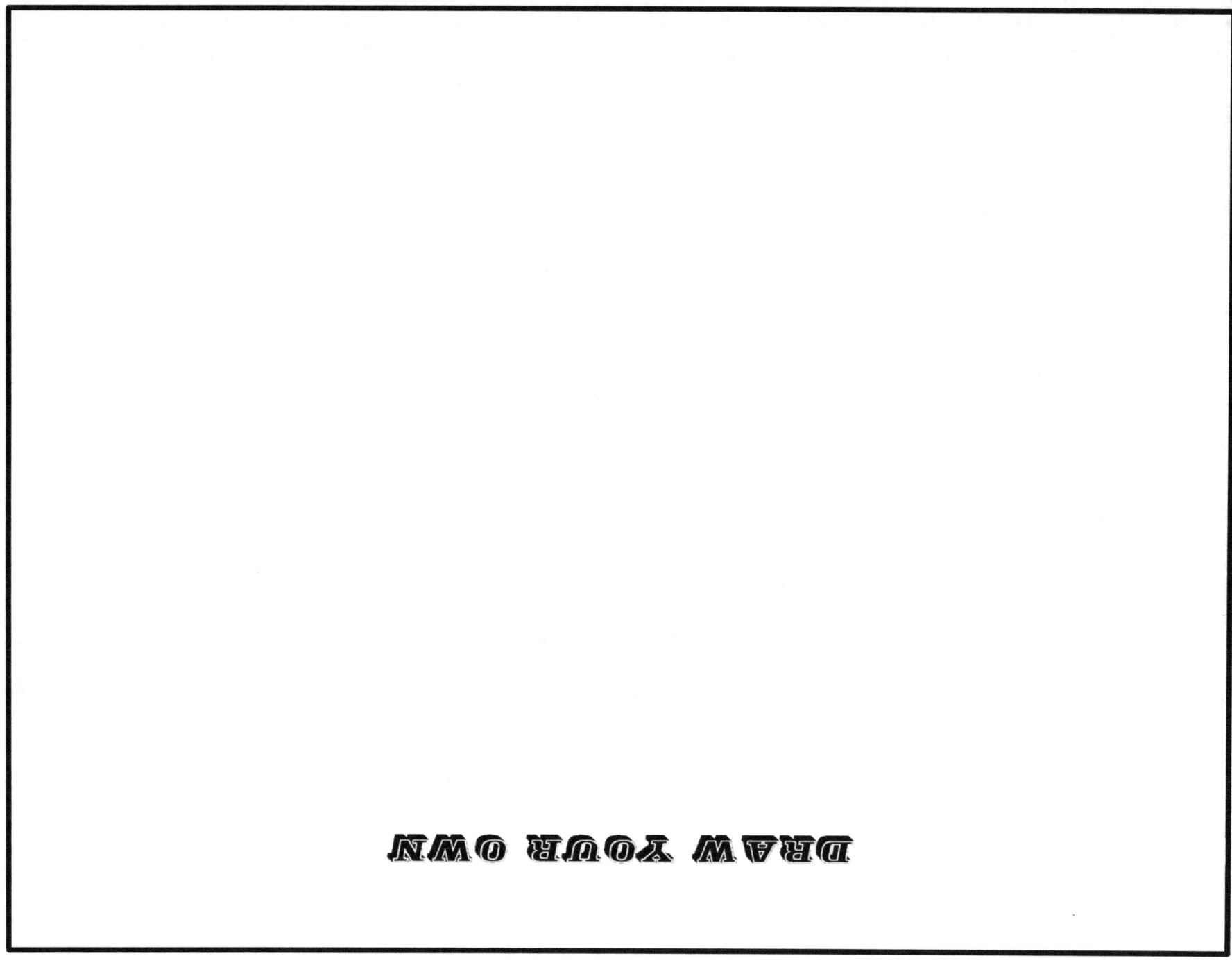

1. Brm Awbbamhdqb Qwdbo smqm wc 1816

   The Littleport Riots were in 1816

2. Ilr kda stkqckqhrtv sx qkb z Lrtsizhr Orqitr

   The old Ironmongery is now a Heritage Centre

3. Uqbob rbob 215 ktseym qgtdbd yw Eyuuebkgou yw 1900

   There were 215 public houses in Littleport in 1900

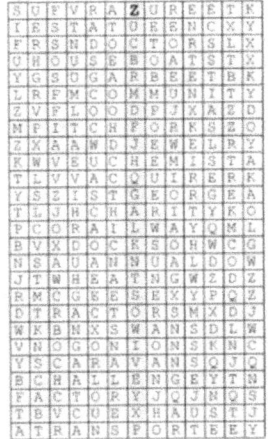

1. ALWPA = SWANS
2. HUQWHK = ROTARY
3. EMWIIDPND = CHALLENGE
4. DPNXPDDHXPN = ENGINEERING
5. QXNGH = TIGER
6. HXUQA = RIOTS
7. AQNDUHND = STGEORGE
8. CUQUHEKEID = MOTORCYCLE

talking
used to be
banned during
working
hours at
the hope
shirt factory
in littleport

7	8	9	2	3	6	1	5	4
6	1	4	5	9	7	2	8	3
3	5	2	4	8	1	7	6	9
5	9	6	3	7	4	8	1	2
4	2	8	1	6	9	3	7	5
1	3	7	2	5	8	9	4	6
8	4	5	9	1	2	6	3	7
9	7	3	6	4	5	8	2	1
2	6	1	7	3	5	4	9	8

1. ALWPA = SWANS
2. HÜOWHK = ROTARY
3. EMWIIDPND = CHALLENGE
4. DPNXPDHXPN = ENGINEERING
5. ÖXNDH = TIGER
6. HXÖÄ = RIOTS
7. AÖNDÜHND = STGEORGE
8. CRÖÜHEKEID = MOTORCYCLE

ypi is dedicated
to the young
people in
littleport

1. 843 8455243 7446 927 6744462559
   3662833 86 843 94 46 1984

   The village sign was originally donated to the
   WI in 1984

2. 46 1947 5488537678 423 2 83774253
   35663

   In 1947 Littleport had a terrible flood

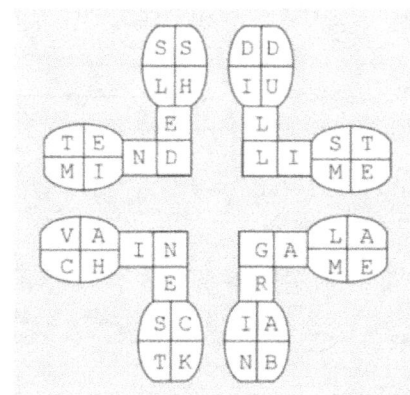

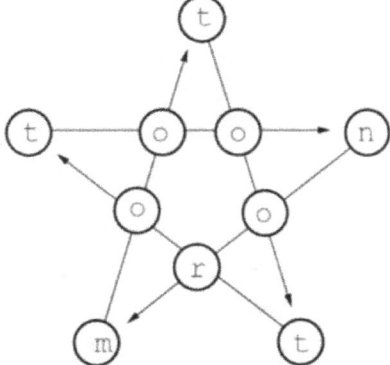

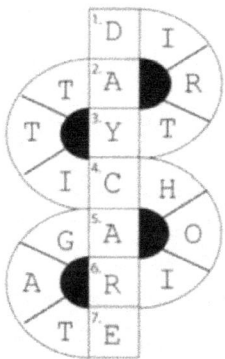

1 to 3: not clean

2 to 4: room under roof

4 to 6: large group of singers

5 to 7: a translucent quartz

1. In a certain code-language, CUL WAP DIR means red little box, SUT MAD BIX means well arranged pile, BIX, FAC, DIR means pile of boxes. What is the code for "of here is"?

   A: FAC
   B: SUT
   C: DIR
   D: BIX

2. In a family there is a husband, wife, two sons and two daughters. All the ladies were invited to a dinner. Both sons went to the park to play, the husband did not return home yet from office. Who was left at home?

   A: Only the wife was at home
   B: All the ladies were at home
   C: Only the sons were at home
   D: Nobody was at home

1. Following is the bus route for Bus Number 10. Buses on this route generally go to Connaught palace. We are inferring that this bus goes to the Connaught place. Choose the correct inference:

   A: The inference is definitely true
   B: The inference is definitely false
   C: The inference can not be drawn

2. If in a code language, COULD is written as BNTKC and MARGIN is written as LZQFHM, how will MOULDING be written in that code?

   A: NITKCMF
   B: CMFINTK
   C: LNKFCMHF
   D: LNTKCMHF

1. S K I D S
   ? 3N 4S 2W
2. W I S E R
   ? 4E 2N 4E 3S
3. D R E A D
   ? 3W 2W 3S 4E
4. H A B I T
   ? 1N 5W 1W 1W
5. A B I D E
   ? 4E 2N 2W 2N

6. A C I D S
   ? 3S 4E 2N 4E
7. G A U G E
   ? 2E 2S 5E 2N
8. M Y R R H
   ? 2N 6W 2N 4E
9. G R O U P
   ? 1N 6W 3N 5E
10. R O U G H
    ? 2E 2S 5W 2S

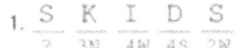

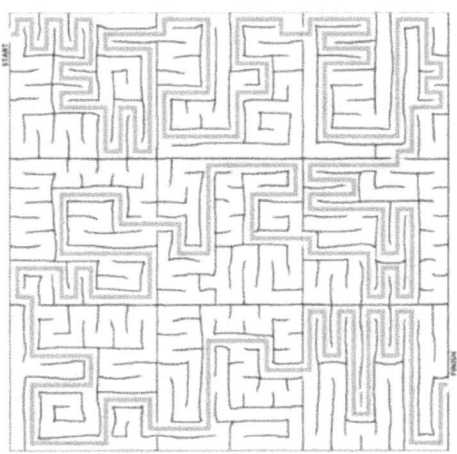

8	1	4	9	2	6	5	3	7
9	6	7	5	3	1	4	2	8
3	5	2	8	7	4	6	1	9
7	8	3	1	4	5	2	9	6
6	2	9	7	8	3	1	4	5
1	4	5	2	6	9	7	8	3
4	3	1	6	9	7	8	5	2
2	9	6	4	5	8	3	7	1
5	7	8	3	1	2	9	6	4

1. In a military code, CAUTION is coded as UACITNO. How will you write MISUNDERSTAND?

   B
   A: SIMUNDSRTAND
   B: SIMNUEDSSRAIDN
   C: SMIUNDERSTAND
   D: None of the above

2. Ms. Forest likes to let her students choose who their partners will be; however, no pair of students may work together more than seven class periods in a row. Adam and Baxter have studied together seven class periods in a row. Carter and Dennis have worked together three class periods in a row. Carter does not want to work with Adam, who should be assigned to work with Baxter?

   A
   A: Carter
   B: Adam
   C: Dennis
   D: Forest